Christopher Columbus

SPIRIT
of America®

CHRISTOPHER *Columbus*

EXPLORER

By Judy Alter

The Child's World®
Chanhassen, Minnesota

6

CHRISTOPHER *Columbus*

Published in the United States of America by The Child's World®
PO Box 326 • Chanhassen, MN 55317-0326 • 800-599-READ • www.childsworld.com

Acknowledgments
The Child's World®: Mary Berendes, Publishing Director

Editorial Directions, Inc.: E. Russell Primm, Emily Dolbear, and Lucia Raatma, Editors; Linda S. Koutris, Photo Selector; Dawn Friedman, Photo Research; Red Line Editorial, Fact Research; Irene Keller, Copy Editor; Tim Griffin/IndexServ, Indexer; Chad Rubel, Proofreader

Photos
Cover: Giraudon/Art Resource, NY; Giraudon/Art Resource, NY: 2, 27; Scala/Art Resource, NY: 23; Vanni/Art Resource, NY: 28; Giraudon/Lauros/ Bridgeman Art Library: 6; Index/Bridgeman Art Library: 7; Library of Congress, Washington, DC/Bridgeman Art Library: 18; Francis G. Mayer/Corbis: 9; Corbis: 17, 22 bottom; Hulton Archive/Getty Images: 8, 12, 14 bottom, 21, 25; North Wind Picture Archives: 14 top, 15, 19, 22 top, 24; Stock Montage: 11, 13, 20, 26.

Registration
The Child's World®, Spirit of America®, and their associated logos are the sole property and registered trademarks of The Child's World®.

Library of Congress Cataloging-in-Publication Data
Alter, Judy, 1938–
  Christopher Columbus : explorer / by Judy Alter.
    p. cm.
Includes index.
Summary: Briefly introduces the life of explorer Christopher Columbus, his accomplishments, and his impact on the world as we know it.
  ISBN 1-56766-161-0 (lib. bdg. : alk. paper)
  1. Columbus, Christopher—Juvenile literature. 2. Explorers—America—Biography—Juvenile literature. 3. Explorers—Spain—Biography—Juvenile literature. 4. America—Discovery and exploration—Spanish—Juvenile literature. [1. Columbus, Christopher. 2. Explorers. 3. America—Discovery and exploration—Spanish.] I. Title.
  E111 .A45 2002
  970.01'5—dc21
                            2001007395

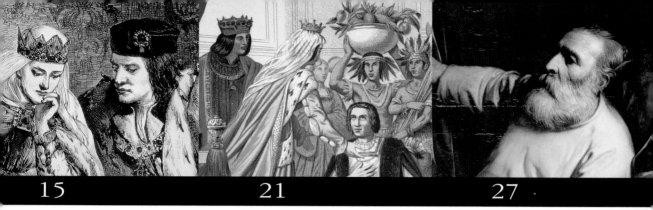

Contents

Chapter ONE

Sailing West

IN THE EARLY 1400S, EUROPEANS TREASURED the silks, gold, and jewelry that came from Asia. Spices, such as pepper, were also popular. But many people believed that the Earth was flat. They thought that if they sailed west to Asia, they would fall off the edge of the Earth!

So European traders and explorers traveled to Asia by going *east*. They made the trip with camels. The Arabs and Turks who controlled the desert did not like Europeans. The trip over the desert was difficult and slow.

This map of the world is a colored engraving from 1486.

By the late 1400s, however, most people had come to believe the Earth was round. An explorer named Christopher Columbus believed that he could sail *west* to Asia. A famous mapmaker told him that the land now called Japan was only 3,000 miles (4,827 kilometers) west. It was really about four times farther away!

Columbus sailed for the Americas with a fleet, or group, of three ships. Two of the ships—the *Niña* and the *Pinta*—were strong enough to cross the ocean but small enough to explore shallow waters. They were called

Christopher Columbus sailed the Pinta, *the* Niña, *and the* Santa María *to the West Indies in 1492.*

Interesting Fact

▶ Although he sailed in the name of Spain, Columbus was Italian by birth.

caravels. The third ship, the *Santa María*, was larger and carried more men.

None of the ships ever touched **mainland** North America. Historians disagree about exactly where the ships landed but they agree that it was an island in the Bahamas, about 400 miles (644 km) southeast of Florida.

On October 12, 1492, Columbus raised the royal flag, claiming for Spain the island he named San Salvador.

Columbus thought he had landed on an island of the East Indies, near Japan or China. Dark-skinned native people came forward to greet him. They were probably peaceful Native American people known as the Taino. Columbus called them "Indians" and he claimed their land for Spain. Then he sailed on and landed on several other islands, including Cuba.

A portrait of Christopher Columbus from the 1500s

Columbus had "discovered" America. He may have been the first European to touch land in the Americas. Certainly he was the most important. After his first voyage, European explorers sailed time and again to North America. Trade began between Europe and the Americas. In this way, Columbus changed the world.

MOST AMERICANS BELIEVE CHRISTOPHER COLUMBUS "DISCOVERED" America. In the United States, we honor Columbus in many ways. We celebrate Columbus Day on the second Monday in October. We have named cities after the explorer, such as Columbus, Ohio; Columbia, South Carolina; and the city of Washington in the District of Columbia. We sing "Hail, Columbia."

In 1893, the United States held an international world's fair to celebrate the 400th anniversary of Columbus landing in the Americas. Called the Columbian Exposition, it was held in Chicago, Illinois (right).

But we know that Columbus and his crew were not the first people on the land now called the United States of America. Many people lived here before his 1492 voyage from Spain.

Tens of thousands of years ago, Asian people came over the Bering land bridge that connected Asia with North America. The descendants of these people are today's Native Americans. Vikings landed in North America. The Portuguese, the Chinese, the Japanese, and others have made claims on this part of the world. Some of these claims may be true; most are probably not true. One thing is certain: Columbus was not the first person to come to the Americas.

Still, it is likely that, in our legends, Columbus will always be the man who "discovered" America. In modern times, people have criticized him for his cruel treatment of Native Americans. He set

an admirable example for adventure and exploration. He also set a less admirable example for cruelty that other Spanish explorers followed.

Christopher Columbus was probably not as noble as the legends have told us. And he was probably not as cruel and mean as he has sometimes been portrayed. Columbus may have been a poor leader of men, but he was a great explorer.

Chapter TWO

An Early Fascination with the Sea

This photograph of Christopher Columbus's house in Genoa, Italy was taken about 1920.

AS A BOY, CHRISTOPHER Columbus was fascinated by the sea. Christopher's given name was Cristoforo Colombo. He was born in the seaport of Genoa, Italy, around 1451.

Christopher had four brothers—Bartholomew, Giovanni Pellegrino, Diego, and Giacomo. He also had one sister named Bianchinetta. Christopher's father was a weaver who traded with the sailing ships that came to the port.

As a young man, Christopher went to sea. At first he carried goods that his father was shipping. Then he became a paid seaman, sailing from Genoa to England. In 1476, ships from France attacked Columbus's ship. He was wounded and thrown into the sea. His ship sank, but he swam safely to shore.

Shortly after that, Christopher Columbus moved to Lisbon, Portugal, where his brother Bartholomew lived. Both brothers worked as chart makers. Although Christopher didn't go to school, he taught himself to speak both Portuguese and Spanish. He also learned **navigation**.

Christopher Columbus in his youth

In 1477, he went to sea again. This time he sailed to England, Ireland, and Iceland. Iceland is closer to America than any other part of Europe. Columbus may have heard about people from Iceland traveling to an unknown land to the west. Today we know that **Vikings** visited North America as early as A.D. 986.

*This drawing shows
the harbor in
Lisbon, Portugal.*

*Christopher Columbus
asked King John II of
Portugal for money for
his voyage.*

Columbus was determined to sail west to
Asia. He asked King John II of Portugal to
pay for a ship and the expenses. The king's
advisers told him not to support the journey.
They thought Columbus did not realize how
large the Earth was. They also believed that
Columbus would be lost at sea, and that
Portugal would lose its money. Columbus
then turned to the governments of
England and France for money. They
refused him, too.

The young Italian explorer then
approached King Ferdinand and Queen
Isabella of Spain. At that time, Portugal
and Spain were great rivals. The Spanish

14

wanted to find a westward route to Asia before the Portuguese. The Spanish also wanted the gold they believed was in this unknown land. They wanted to spread their religion too. But they had no money. Twice King Ferdinand and Queen Isabella turned

King Ferdinand and Queen Isabella of Spain funded Columbus's trip.

Columbus down. They gave him a small amount of money to live on, however.

Columbus waited seven years, selling maps and charts for a living. Legend says that, in 1492, Queen Isabella sold her jewels to support the exploration. Actually, the Spanish government collected on back debts to pay for Christopher Columbus's voyage.

15

WHEN CHRISTOPHER COLUMBUS MADE HIS FIRST VOYAGE, EUROPEANS were just beginning to chart a ship's course by the position of the stars in the sky. Columbus sailed by an older method known as "dead reckoning."

With this method, a ship started from a familiar spot, such as the departure port. The navigator then measured his course and distance from that spot on a chart. Each day's ending position was the starting point for the next day.

To make these measurements, Columbus had to know the speed and direction of the ship. He used a compass to determine direction and an hourglass to measure time. He kept track of the information on a navigational chart (right).

To measure the ship's speed, sailors threw a piece of wood in the water at a mark on the forward deck. The pilot began to chant. He stopped chanting when the wood reached a mark on the back deck. Then he wrote down the last note he chanted. A chart helped him figure the time from these notes.

Another method was to make evenly spaced knots on a long piece of rope. Then the sailors threw the rope overboard. They counted the number of knots drawn overboard in a specific time. The speed of a ship is still measured in knots per hour due to this technique.

Chapter THREE

A Great Hero

WHEN COLUMBUS AND HIS CREW SAILED ON August 3, 1492, people gave them an emotional send-off. They were certain they would never see these men again.

Christopher Columbus was the first sailor known to have kept a logbook, or log. A log is a detailed record of a ship's speed and progress during a voyage. Only the log of Columbus's first voyage still exists. Some say he had two logbooks. The first made the distance seem much shorter so he

King Ferdinand and Queen Isabella see Columbus off from the dock on August 3, 1492.

showed that one to the crew. The second logbook gave the true distances.

On October 12, 1492, the crew spotted land and went ashore. Columbus claimed to be the first to sight land. Others say it was one of his sailors on another ship.

When Columbus set sail again, he took a few Taino Indians

In this drawing, a Taino chief addresses Columbus in what is now Cuba.

with him as guides. The party eventually landed in what is now Cuba. Columbus expected to find gold. He thought he had landed at Cathay, which was the European name for northern China at that time.

Instead of gold, the Native Americans gave Columbus a dried weed called tobacco. They set fire to small pieces of it and breathed in the smoke. Columbus took the weed back to Spain.

Interesting Fact

▶ Columbus brought tobacco to Europe on his first voyage and horses to the Americas on his second voyage.

The Santa María
was wrecked on
December 25, 1492.

Columbus then sailed on to present-day Haiti, which he named Hispaniola. He believed he had reached Japan. The Haitians had gold and shared it generously. Columbus also filled his ships with exotic birds, herbs, spices—and a few prisoners.

On Christmas Day, the *Santa María* ran aground. Columbus ordered his men to save supplies and leave the ship. When he sailed back to Spain, he had to leave 20 men behind because there was no room for them on the remaining ships. He left them in a settlement he called La Navidad.

The rest of the crew returned to Spain on March 15, 1493. Ferdinand and Isabella were pleased with what Columbus brought from the Americas. They showered him with gifts and honors. He was praised throughout Spain as a great hero.

The Spanish king and queen willingly gave Columbus money for a much larger exploration. On September 25, 1493,

Columbus set sail again with 17 ships and more than 1,200 men. On this second voyage, Columbus touched land at Dominica in the West Indies and at Puerto Rico, which was then called Borinquén.

Then he sailed on to La Navidad, where he had left some of his men. He found that many of the men left behind had died of sickness, and the Native Americans had

Christopher Columbus brought Native Americans and goods to the Spanish court in 1493.

This drawing shows the Native Americans killing the Spanish settlers of La Navidad.

La Isabela was abandoned in 1496 after an outbreak of disease. Some of the graves are still there today.

killed the others when they asked for food. Columbus then killed the Indian leaders and sent many others back to Spain as slaves.

Columbus made himself governor of Hispaniola. He built a settlement and named it La Isabela, in honor of the Spanish queen. He wanted La Isabela to be a trading post for Europeans and Asian powers. Columbus still believed he was near China and expected to see Chinese **pagodas** and arched bridges. When he didn't find them, he returned to Spain in 1496. He left his brothers, Diego and Bartholomew, in charge of La Isabela. After food shortages and an outbreak of disease, La Isabela was abandoned. Bartholomew founded a new settlement called Santo Domingo.

This time, Columbus returned to Spain with very little gold. Ferdinand and Isabella were disappointed by his small treasures and his violent treatment of the Native Americans.

Columbus was able to persuade the king and queen to pay for a third voyage, however. They thought surely he could find more gold. By then, France and Spain were at war.

SOME PEOPLE MAY IMAGINE THAT COLUMBUS SAILED IN HUGE SHIPS WITH hundreds of men. In fact, only 90 men accompanied him on his first voyage. They were all seasoned sailors from Spain, though.

At one time, many people believed Columbus's sailors were all cut-throats and former criminals. The Spanish government had been afraid

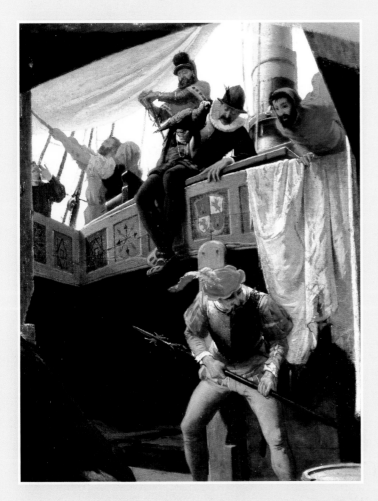

Columbus could not raise a crew so they offered freedom to criminals who were interested. In the end, however, only four criminals were on the three ships. One was a murderer, and the other three had helped him escape from prison. Historians have been able to identify 87 members of the crew of the first voyage.

On that voyage, the master and pilots were paid 2,000 *maravedis* a month, or about $200 in today's money. Able seamen were paid $100, and ordinary seamen earned about $65.

Because the ships were small, more than 40 men lived in one dark, **musty** room. The room was about 70 to 80 feet (21 to 24 m) long with a 6-foot (1.8-m) ceiling. There was no water for bathing, of course, and many sailors developed a disease called **scurvy** due to the lack of fresh vegetables and fruits.

Chapter FOUR

Final Return to Spain

Columbus returned to Spain in chains and met with King Ferdinand and Queen Isabella.

IN 1498, COLUMBUS SET SAIL FROM SPAIN with six ships. Three of the ships carried food and supplies for the Santo Domingo settlement on Hispaniola. There he found that his brothers had imprisoned more Indians and

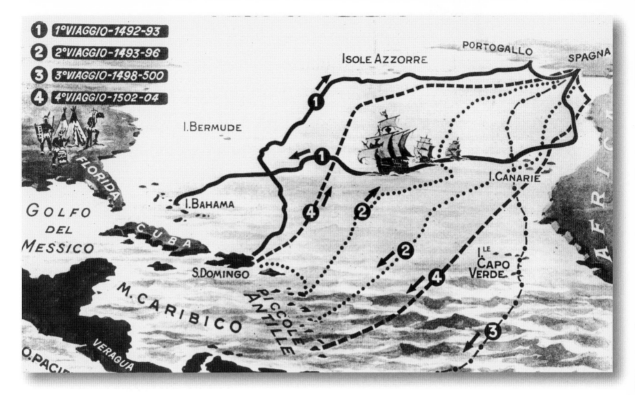

1º VIAGGIO – 1492-93
2º VIAGGIO – 1493-96
3º VIAGGIO – 1498-500
4º VIAGGIO – 1502-04

ISOLE AZZORRE
PORTOGALLO
SPAGNA
I.BERMUDE
FLORIDA
GOLFO DEL MESSICO
CUBA
I.BAHAMA
I.CANARIE
S.DOMINGO
PICCOLE ANTILLE
M. CARIBICO
I LE CAPO VERDE
AFRICA
O.PACI
VERAGUA

This map shows the four voyages of Christopher Columbus.

had also reorganized the distribution of gold. Some Spaniards received more gold than others and rebellious Spaniards had been killed. In his efforts to restore order, Columbus killed more rebel leaders.

The king and queen of Spain learned about the disorder on Hispaniola. They sent someone to investigate the cruelty against the Native Americans and the greed of Columbus and his brothers. The chief justice took Columbus and his brothers into custody and sent them back to Spain in chains.

Ferdinand and Isabella immediately ordered the chains removed, but chose

Interesting Fact

▶ Columbus met and married a Portuguese woman in 1478. Their son, Diego, was born the next year. Five years later, Columbus's wife died.

Queen Isabella is shown here writing her will before she died.

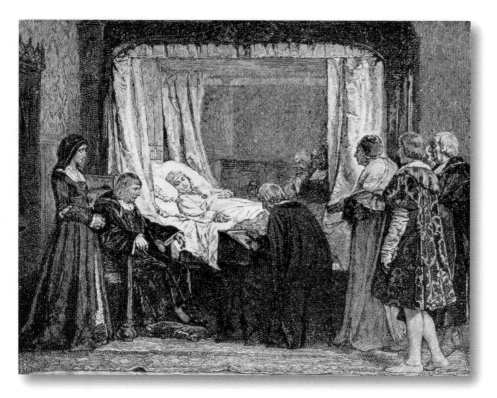

another man to govern Hispaniola. While they appreciated Columbus's skill as an explorer, they questioned his ability as a leader. By 1502, Christopher Columbus had won his property and honors back. He was permitted to sail on a fourth voyage. Columbus called his last trip the High Voyage because he thought it would bring back the fame he had once enjoyed. He sailed from Spain on May 9, 1502.

Columbus stopped at Hispaniola and then sailed south past Jamaica, Cuba, Honduras, and Nicaragua. The voyage was difficult, however. Rains were heavy, and the Indians were unfriendly. Finally, in defeat, Columbus headed back to Hispaniola. But this time, his ships were unable to reach the island. The

This painting shows Columbus just before his death in 1506.

wooden ships leaked from worm and insect holes. He and his crew spent almost a year in Jamaica before ships sent from Hispaniola rescued them. Then they returned to Spain.

In Spain, Columbus learned that Queen Isabella was near death. King Ferdinand did not have her passion for exploration so there was no interest in sending Columbus to sea again.

Columbus was about 55 years old, but his health was poor. He suffered from **arthritis**, and he had been sick with **malaria**. He spent the last year of his life in Spain an unhappy man. He felt that he had not been given the credit or the wealth he deserved. Christopher Columbus died on May 20, 1506.

This monument in Seville, Spain, contains part of the remains of Christopher Columbus.

Columbus was buried in a church in Valladolid, Spain. Later, his remains were moved to the family tomb in Seville, Spain. His final resting place is in the Cathedral of Santo Domingo in Hispaniola. There he is buried next to his son, Diego.

Christopher Columbus will be remembered as one of the most important explorers in history. His voyages to the Americas changed the world forever.

1451 Christopher Columbus is born in Genoa, Italy. His given name is Cristoforo Colombo.

1476 Columbus joins his brother, Bartholomew, in Lisbon, Portugal.

1477–1482 Columbus makes trading voyages and visits Iceland and other lands.

1485 Columbus moves to Spain.

1492 Columbus sets sail from Palos, Spain, with the *Niña*, the *Pinta*, and the *Santa María*. He and his crew land somewhere in the Bahamas. Columbus stops in Cuba and Hispaniola, and founds a settlement he names La Navidad.

1493 Columbus sails back to Spain. He then sets off on a second voyage and returns to Hispaniola. He finds La Navidad destroyed. He then builds a settlement named La Isabela.

1494 Columbus sails to Cuba, Jamaica, Hispaniola, and then returns to La Isabela.

1496 Columbus departs for Spain, leaving his brothers in charge of La Isabela.

1498 Columbus leaves Spain with six ships on his third voyage.

1500 Upon learning of the disorder in Hispaniola, the king and queen of Spain order an investigation. Columbus and his brothers are returned to Spain in chains.

1502 With his honor and property restored, Columbus sails with four ships on his fourth and final voyage.

1504 Columbus returns to Spain for the last time.

1506 Columbus dies at age 55 in Valladolid, Spain.

Glossary TERMS

arthritis (ar-THRYE-tiss)
Arthritis is a disease that makes a person's joints swollen and sore. Columbus suffered from arthritis when he got older.

caravels (KA-ruh-vels)
Caravels are small sailing ships that were common in the 1500s. The *Niña* and the *Pinta* were caravels.

mainland (MAYN-lahnd)
The largest piece of land that makes up a country is called the mainland. Neither the *Niña*, nor the *Pinta*, nor the *Santa María* touched mainland North America on Columbus's first voyage.

malaria (muh-LAYR-ee-uh)
Malaria is a serious tropical disease carried by mosquitoes. Columbus suffered from malaria when he was an older man.

musty (MUHSS-tee)
When something is musty, it smells of dampness and decay. Rooms on Columbus's ships were often musty.

navigation (nav-ih-GAY-shun)
Navigation is the use of maps, compasses, or the stars to chart a course on a trip. Columbus learned navigation early in life.

pagodas (puh-GO-duhs)
Pagodas are temples used in Eastern religions. Pagodas often have many roofs that curl upward.

scurvy (SKUR-vee)
Scurvy is a disease that is caused by lack of vitamin C, which is found in fruits and vegetables. People with scurvy often have bleeding gums and are very weak.

Vikings (VY-kings)
The Vikings were seafaring people from Scandinavia who invaded the coasts of Britain. Vikings visited North America as early as A.D. 986.

For Further INFORMATION

Web Sites

Visit our homepage for lots of links about Christopher Columbus:
http://www.childsworld.com/links.html

Note to Parents, Teachers, and Librarians:
We routinely verify our Web links to make sure they're safe,
active sites—so encourage your readers to check them out!

Books

Chrisp, Peter. *Christopher Columbus, Explorer of the New World.* New York: Dorling Kindersley, 2001.

Fritz, Jean. *Where Do You Think You're Going, Christopher Columbus?* New York: Putnam and Grosset, 1997.

Gallagher, Carole. *Christopher Columbus and the Discovery of the New World.* Bromall, Penn.: Chelsea House Publishers, 1999.

Yolen, Jane. *Encounter.* New York: Harcourt Brace, 1992.

Places to Visit or Contact

The Mariners' Museum
To see exhibits about navigators
100 Museum Drive
Newport News, VA 23606
757-596-2222

Corpus Christi Museum of Science and History
To see Spanish-built reproductions of Columbus's three ships that commemorated the 500th anniversary of Columbus's voyages to the Americas
1900 North Chaparral Street
Corpus Christi, TX 78401
361-883-2862

Index